MISTER GOODBYE
EASTER ISLAND

MISTER GOODBYE
EASTER ISLAND

Jon Woodward

ALICE JAMES BOOKS
FARMINGTON, MAINE

for my teachers, with love and thanks

10 9 8 7 6 5 4 3 2 1

Alice James Books are published by Alice James Poetry Cooperative, Inc.,
an affiliate of the University of Maine at Farmington.

Alice James Books
238 Main Street
Farmington, ME 04938

www.alicejamesbooks.org

Library of Congress Cataloging-in-Publication Data
Woodward, Jon, 1978-
  Mister goodbye Easter Island / Jon Woodward.
     p. cm.
  ISBN 1-882295-42-0
  I. Title.
  PS3623.O685M57 2003
  811'.6--dc21

                              2003011212

Alice James Book gratefully acknowledges support from the University of
Maine at Farmington and the National Endowment for the Arts. ❦

Cover art: Todd McKie, "You Think You've Got Problems," Courtesy of
the artist and Clark Gallery, Lincoln, MA. Photo: David Caras.

ACKNOWLEDGEMENTS

Grateful acknowledgement is made to the editors of the following publications in which these poems first appeared, sometimes in earlier versions:

The Canary River Review:
"And Because the Leaves Were On Strike"
"In Silence"

can we have our ball back?:
"All the Better"
"Two Hawks Are Above Cambridge"
"Upwards"
"What I Can Make Out From Here"
"Where Billy Goats Should Always Stay, Too"

I'd like to thank Patrick Hargon, Lisa Hargon-Smith, Arda Collins, Jon-Lizzie-Dash-Foley-Wilkins, Katie Peterson, Jeremy Noel-Tod, Marc Flynn, Tonya Kisner, Tony Ioanna, Sarah Manguso, April Ossmann and everyone at Alice James Books, Ryan and Amy Spoering, Michael McCarthy, Shadd Wade, Peter and Cindy Woodward, Anne Woodward, and many many others, for their support of this book. Thanks to Vermont Studio Center, for the space and time. I am especially grateful to Oni Buchanan, one million times.

CONTENTS

SECTION ONE

Auditioning Anchormen

There were clowns and armpits
and clowns and arm
pits and there were window
washers arm wrestling each other
and armpits and there was one

odd little man in the corner
whose white bones glowed
when a shadow passed over him

whose body had clearly
been wandering forever in the desert,
tripping over its own bleached skull
every twenty years or so

At the Mythical Beast

We have gathered around the Mythical Beast, to discuss it
and its future. Some of us are spelling Mythical with a k:
Mythickal. I think that looks dirty. The funding for the
Mythical Beast is drying up, and we are discussing the future,
because now is the time. We can't afford the thorn polish
anymore, and are forced to concoct a lame-duck, all-purpose
polish: 50% thorn polish, 40% hoof polish, 10% Tabasco
sauce. There is considerable tarnish on all parts, resultantly.
We want to throw a tarp over it, to hide its entarnishment, but
we can scarcely afford that much canvas. The time to call the
Mythical Beast out of its slumber is upon us, according to some
gathered here. Others think that would be a disaster. That's
what we're discussing at this meeting.

Alternatives to awakening the Beast:

"We could open a soda fountain in the belly of the Beast. We
    would sell soda and malted milk."
"Nobody wants to buy malted milk, they want politics."
"Buying malted milk is a political act."
"Toppling monuments is a political act, shall we then topple the
    Beast?"
"Shall we then enter the Beast into a run for political office?"
"Standing in the amusement park motionlessly is a political
    act."
"Standing motionlessly maintaining secrets. Maintenance, and
    saying nothing."
"There is room enough in the belly of the Beast to fit a whole
    amusement park in the belly of the Beast."
"A marriage of perception and intuition."
"You have to spend money to make money."
"We can strap more and more pieces of gadgetry to the Beast,
    so that they, the pieces, dangle therefrom."
"What will be the profit?"
"Dangling is its own profit, according to my . . . "

"Can the Beasssssst be made to ssssssspeak?"
"What stories could it tell?"
"Who would publish the Beast's stories?"
"Our own presssssssssss. Mythickal Presssssssssss."
"Mythickal with a k?"
"Yesssssssssssssssss."
"Oh no. We haven't got the funding for a k."

The fellow with the lisssssp seems to have appeared out of nowhere, in the very middle of the conversation. We haven't seen him at any of the meetings before. Neither was he recorded on any of the security tapes from any of the Beast's eyes. The Beast has 40 eyes and sees in every direction. Seeing all is a political act. Seeing all and saying nothing.

"Awakening the Beast is a political act, there can be no denying it. Hey, anyone see where that green-skinned fella with the speech impediment went to?"
"A golf course, on the back of the Beast?"
"A municipal airport, on the back of the Beast?"
"Maybe we're going about this the wrong way. We're trying to turn the Beast into something it's not, and maybe that's going about it the wrong way."
"So that's it, is it?"
"I'm just saying, is all."
"So that's it?"
"I'm just saying."

This line of conversation, the tone and the tension in the air, begins to awaken the Mythical Beast. Several of us detect a stirring of the feathers. A redirection of the conversation is necessary:

"A pillow talk."
"A puppet show."
"The sanguine metropolis."
"Metropolis polish."
"A lull."

"A helping of gravy."

The energy of the conversation was safely diffused, then. We must all be careful and vigilant. This Beast is a thing of terror we haven't got the scope to comprehend. Having said that, what are we going to do with it?

The Eel and the Breaking Point

"I am not an eel," said the eel.
"If I had hands, though, I would play
the same three chords over
and over and over. And
what are you? What
are you supposed
to do?"

The breaking point chuckled
through his gray eyes and sighed
and said, "Never fear, I shall not tread
on you directly." He gazed at the ether,
free and clear, exactly unlike piano wire.
Again he sighed, "Eel,
this will be the ether, thy mother;
and I will be thy father."

The eel frowned sideways and said,
"I don't see anything there.
And I'm not an eel." The eel was not
introspective. He needed to eat, to grow
hands, to fashion a box
with hammers and piano wire in it,
to chop down ivory trees.
True, ivory trees tend to outrun or
trample hunters, or go extinct sometimes,
but the eel flexed his ribbony muscles
and all those problems shrank to singularities,
and time itself went dark for a moment.
He made his phrase-coining face, then,
and spat a fat phrase into the void.

That was it.
The breaking point positioned himself and sighed.
Now he would do what he had come to do.

The Punchline Is . . .

My duck followed me on board my spacecraft, the *Bossa Nova*.
He has a thing for pushing buttons and flapping around in zero-
gravity.

The artificial gravity is expensive so I only turn it on in certain
rooms: the ship's beach room, and the ship's chapel.

My duck likes to follow me into the beach room and get sand
kicked in his face by the automatic bully. Then he likes to
follow me into the chapel and push the chaplain's buttons.

Between times, he cocks his brainless little head and stares out
the windows at the void.

His lighthearted waterfowl soul seems somewhat colored by
thoughts of death ever since boarding the *Bossa Nova*. He keeps
on pushing the death button. Fortunately, that button's not
hooked up to anything.

Where Billy Goats Should Always Stay, Too

A little man dangled from ropes and helped out in the daycare center. He kept his eyes on the tracks that ran through the daycare center when a train was coming. He wanted to keep the children safe from the trains.

Young Jane was on the tracks this time. The little man swooped down on his ropes and snatched up Young Jane just before the train would have hit her. Then his ropes pulled them both to safety.

He knelt down in front of Young Jane and said, "Young Jane, you shouldn't play on the tracks. Little girls should always stay on the platform." Young Jane said, "I wasn't a little girl, it was one of my transformations. I was a billy goat."

The little man said, "Billy goats should always stay on the platform, too." He pointed his finger down the platform at a billy goat that was standing there. "See?"

All the Better

Little Red Riding Hood starts at one end of the hood with the intention of making it to the other. When I say "starts" I mean walking. It's the hood-end of the hood she starts at. It's a gaping hole that will surely engulf her.
"My! what a gaping hole you have."
"All the better to engulf you with."
Which it does.

Grandma has also been eaten. Grandma begins a journey across the intestinal landscape.

Inside the hole of the hood, LRRH finds a wolf dressed in a red riding hood. "Aren't you supposed to be in my Grandmother's clothes?" But the wolf unzips and really he's a red hood wearing a red hood. "So the sun is setting over the red hills, and the clothes are wearing themselves," LRRH says, by way of soliloquy.

Grandma is oil painting. Grandma is interviewing herself. Grandma hits the bottle. Grandma hangs herself from a door-way inside the Big Bad Wolf.

LRRH continues: "I haven't made it very far into the mystery of the hood. I wish that my name was not the garment I wear, the same as my garment's name. I wish it was not the mystery I have been given to investigate. My! what a big mess it all is." This, outside the house she's knocking on the door of. The Big Bad Wolf, dressed in the clothing of every possible name other than his own, answers the door.

First Ending (Dressed in the Next Ending's Clothes): Once upon a time this story ended simply, the wolf ate everybody. But at a certain historical moment, the story changed, as though its body had grown a new limb, out of which a Lumberjack sprang fully dressed and fully grown and hacked the wolf to pieces. Then, about 1945, the Lumberjack began skinning the wolf and keeping the hide for himself, just in case.

Next Ending (Dressed in the Next Next Ending's Clothes): When the Big Bad Wolf answers the door the Lumberjack springs up like a paper target and chops open the wolf. Then the wolf chops open the Lumberjack.

"Stop it," one says to the other.

"You stop it yourself."

"I can't stop."

What I Realized About the Dog-Rabbit

I started into a labyrinth and I dropped sandwiches behind me.
The sandwiches were little selves.

Would I had kept the little selves on my little shelves.

Why, I've never seen such a yellow labyrinth,
it's like the outside of a school bus in here, is what I said.

It occurred to me:

It's a bus full of children, that dog-rabbit!
When it eats me it's eating a sandwich.

I am a door and bee sandwich.

I'm teaching your children pattern recognition skills.
I go door, then bee, then door, then bee . . .

When the Dog Is Chasing You

Oh the night is dog enough
When the dog is chasing you
Oh the legs can't fast enough
When the dog's lambasting you

Oh the river's wide enough
When the dog's in the bank with you
Oh the hide ain't hide enough
When the dog's outflanking you

Oh the stairs don't climb enough
When the dog is sniffing you
Oh the guns ain't sublime enough
For the hell that dog is giving you

Oh no thoughts are loud enough
To swat that dog with reason
Oh no years are long enough
That dog owns every season

God said that little boys gotta run
And dogs gotta make them afraid
But I prayed to God to kill that dog
"God, kill that dog" I prayed

Ascension of Worm

The food stamp I found in the parking lot was a leaf.
It took me in with its red and yellow.

Etched nowhere on it was a stick figure
being beheaded by a Hooded Beheader.
Neither head nor Beheader was pictured

yet the verb of the beheading was.
The leaf was edited for content.

I walked up the stairs into the empty church.
The silence there was like the sound of adjustment,
the building getting used to its own medium.

What I found in the parking lot was possibly an astronaut,
now that I've measured his trajectory.

It's death, going up in a rocket, I've heard.
It's not like slithering at all: cramming
yourself between layers of air

down (up) into the all-hole.
I'm still getting used to being an "astronaut" myself.

All I have so far is the white worm suit,
from which not even my face protrudes.
Someone lassoes me and yanks

me toward heaven, above the clouds
into divine light, sweet and antibacterial,

I feel my halves bulging,
everything is so quiet here,
the silvery braid is sliding through me.

Angels

I am engulfed in a swarm of angels, I'm watching them move around me in slow motion. I have disturbed their hive. They move in a golden light that comes from them, I think. They're like a school of fish that makes its own water. I feel like I'm at the center of a whirlpool. The angels can't touch me. They are angry, and they move around me, but they can't touch me.

SECTION TWO

Jacques Cousteau Goes to All the Trouble

"You got any threes?" (I need threes.
His expression, like his blue knit cap,
doesn't change.) "Go fish,"
he says. No wait, I think
it's supposed to be vice versa,
he's supposed to go fish.
Oh, I've ruined everything.
I'll just go and jump off a bridge, again.

Thankfully there seems to be no body of water
I can lose my marbles into
that Cousteau won't fish them out of again.
In fact, in the movie "Jacques Cousteau vs. Harry Houdini,"
when Harry stepped out of the deadly water,
dripping and free of his shackles,
Cousteau came out the way he went in.
He was wet and free to begin with.
We're led to understand this is why he won in the end.

It's not enough that he owns his own boat?
Let's say I bust my nose surfing somewhere,
you think Houdini's coming to my rescue?
Cousteau can smell blood in the water
and he'll come growing extra rows of teeth
circling me with his fins outswept and making airplane noises,
challenging all comers. Let's say the knot on my nose
gets big as a dolphin's eye, let's say
I hold my head back to stop the bleeding,
and I see the Lord's own horizon like a black circle around me,
with the Lord's own full moon like a fat pearl
collecting layers in the sky. Do you think
all the concentric circles make a lick of difference?

Method Acting

Thor Heyerdahl Jr. is in the cool basement, scrutinizing
all previous scrutiny.
There is the sound of suds.
His project will fail, no question.

Look at the lad, braced as he is against
a hand-made washtub modeled
after the washtubs of a non-existent tribe
of people, scrubbing the frog suit

which is their tribal garment and which he wears
to discover their secrets. The years
have washed away the secrets like Cadillacs
made of sand. He stands in his boxer shorts.

It's important to log time out of the frog suit,
if only when cleaning it, to run
his fingers along the green terrycloth seams,
looking for holes, meaning,

where there were not holes before. It's
crucial to come to see the eyes of the suit
again as cloth eyes, not staring eyes,
not gleaming with the light of mischief

in the bathroom mirror at 2 a.m., deeply important
to hang it out to dry, have a cup of coffee, a deep
breath, but most important is to zip
himself back into it again, even though

the frog-people never existed and had no
culture or lifestyle to study, and he knows it:
a failure. To zip, even though the results of any inquiry
into inquiry are inherently suspect:

another failure. To zip, even though the reddish stains
never seem to come out of the frog suit:
sigh. How did they do it, he thinks,
how did the frog-people get their stains out?

How did they come to know their own analyses?
And who taught them what dying out is like, if
there was only one of them? And if more than one,
who was in charge of the dying out?

Rasputin as Roboticist

For math, Rasputin needn't use his head:
his abaci could fill a swimming pool.
His bread thief keeps him well supplied with bread;
his serf thief serves him well as well. Raspu-
tin's suit of armor and his yellow duck-
lings follow one another through his halls.
The engine of Rasputin's ladder truck
is well-tuned by his golem of crystal balls.
His Song and Dance Brigade is powered through
his electromagnetism, his tides
(that bathe his shores), his dung beetle, his flu,
his sodium. He's harnessed many brides,
and many ready wombs, many Matterhorns,
and many climbers dying to be unborn.

Thor Heyerdahl Jr. with Cold Feet

Why not make him insane? How about OCD?
Undue worshipfulness? Something. Something seems right.
He's in the basement. He's working on something.
Then his father needs to come blazing down the stairs.

At first he was dressed up in that frog suit.
He was studying the ways of the frog people. Remember?
He stood in a bucket of water for three days.
It was a rite of passage.

"God damn these quatrains," he says.
He's washing the red stains out of the suit
and checking for holes. How did they
get their stains out? What suits did they

dress up in to study what people? Did they?
His father is sailing across a homemade ocean with fatigued pectorals.
Both father's and son's pectorals are fatigued, they're hurrying.
Now father is landing, now leaving footprints up the beach.

Quickly now son is casting ancient gambling cubes,
asking for answers to ancient questions.
Now father will be pouring down the stairs like jellied fire,
hollering clean up this mess goddammit. He needs to do that.

Poem About How Groucho Marx Is Everywhere These Days

Groucho Marx is not at the supermarket.
Worse:
his eyes are rolling up to heaven,
his leg jerks out from underneath him
under its own power, he
tells me he never forgets a . . .
I'm sorry, what is it he never . . .
but in my case he'll make an exception?

He says if he held me any closer,
we would become phantoms—mist and shoelaces—
and pass through each other.
He would leave glasses and grease paint
on me, and I would make him skinny.
Then we would be behind each other.

And, maybe his body would pace away from me,
clutch, collapse, and die—
I'll no longer have to draw when he says draw,
or when he draws.

Howard McNear Making Love to Two Women

Howard McNear says "quack" but he's aching like a fungus.
Howard McNear, who played Floyd the Barber
  on the Andy Griffith Show,
is buckling like a belt around a pair of planets
in mutual orbit, one good and one evil,
though which is which depends on which planet's encyclopedia
you read, but it doesn't matter, Howard McNear is coming to a boil.
Howard McNear is cooking potatoes with his powerful brain waves,
in his mind, and the twenty-parted crutch system Andy Griffith
rigged to hold up his body is holding it up,
and the barber's chair meant to conceal the thorn in his flesh
from the cameras conceals it, and he's delivering his lines
like he's throwing hard-boiled eggs
at a boat race, or like a videorecording of that act
being sped up and slowed down—in other words
like the twisting of a knob—that easy—
but all of this is just a premonition of what will become,
in his future, his only fantasies, without
the premonition of what the fantasies are trying to escape.
He doesn't know what else to say but "quack,"
or what else to do but ache, and achingly gather
his arms around two of the nakedest
women ever seen in San Diego, which is where they are;
young, horizontal people, years beforehand, in the present,
skins covered over with buttons labeled
"Push Me Again," which, when pushed, play back
Howard McNear's tin-and-tarnish voice,
and one good and one evil female voice, intoning, "Push Me Again."
They do. God bless you, Howard McNear. Have a good life.

The Lucite Pranksters

The best-sellingest hopper takes a seat on a heap of umbrage,
opposite Howard McNear, who played Floyd the Barber
on the Andy Griffith show, and the Lucite Pranksters
are stabbing and stabbing,
and of necessity the chart-topping hopper
heads for the gangplank door,
receding down and down into the floor,
below which is another angry little pile
with another Howard "Floyd" McNear sitting on it,
holding it down, and another pair
of the Lucite Pranksters with another pair of golden dirks,
with which they dirk and dirk—

Cello

Cello is the bird nobody wanted
but I probably have that backwards
having read it off a sign in the dark
on a freight train heading
backwards against the moon
and even though I wrote it down
right away I was using my index
finger to write with and it was dark
and my handwriting isn't great

then they held Cello at gunpoint
on TV for my benefit
and made it confess I am
the bird nobody wanted
and now I just don't know what to think

The Life of Groucho as an Elephant
Lived Backwards

When he's old they take a rifle
and they place it against his ear.
I think I heard a certain sound;
what did Groucho hear?

He snuffles through the bones
of his former fellow Marxes.
Why is it that Groucho
is so interested in carcasses?

At the festival of Groucho
they play games of tug o' war.
Thunderous Groucho bests
and topples eighty men or more.

The woman on his neck
is what he calls his Sweet Mahout;
through his baggy skin he feels
her, like a sack of tender fruit.

Men find a herd of Groucho
and they rope a 5-year-old's legs.
The spirit is the thing inside
that eventually begs.

His mother shits him out and he
lies helpless in the dirt.
The standing, the staggering,
even the sudden air hurts.

Elegy

Did Martin Luther really say "sin boldly?"
The sun, our sun, is frowning down the sky,
sharpening a spoon and blasting, rather coldly,
its light. And Martin Luther is dead. If I
sin boldly like I did this afternoon,
attempting necromancy at his grave,
to what extent will God's angelic goon
squad thrash me as a result? Shouldn't they leave
a few of my bones unbroken so that the next
time I sin so boldly they'll have more
of me to break? I wish I had fewer necks.
And spines. I don't like pain. This isn't fair—
Undead Luther won't pop up like I wanted.
(last line goes here) (God this incantation's slanted)

SECTION THREE

A Field Guide to the Jesuses of North America

INTRODUCTION

For this edition of the Guide I have added at least three or four new features which I think every one of you will enjoy and find puzzling if not entirely useful. One of my favorite things about writing introductions is that it gives me a chance to lean back on my lean and rippling haunches. The pages are in sequential order. Every illustration belongs somewhere and there is a devastating lack of illustrations. The whole thing is crystal clear. I am proud of the work I've done. I am proud of my lean and rippling haunches.

CAJUN-STYLE JESUS

This is how you feel the hours and seconds slipping away. This is your molten life, being drawn into a fine thread no longer capable of supporting its own weight. The Cajun-Style Jesus is a threadbare monster. He is separated into trade payables and expense payables. He is customized. He is eighty-four people.

CASH OR CREDIT ONLY JESUS

The Cash or Credit Only Jesus has a whole mess of electrodes. He is a no-show. He lives in a fort made of five broken pianos. He has taken measures against frostbite, but further measures will have to be taken before the waltz is over. He is a baritone. Usually his voice is described using a color, like "golden" or "violet." How angry is he? Can his anger be described using a color, like "orange," or some other? Does that seem like a misstep?

CHOCOLATE-COVERED JESUS

Habitat stridently, lovely Chocolate-Covered Jesus. Well known to the chocolate moss of underlogs and monogogs, it is a covered lover. To mate one, to the actual deity, to where it lives. It lives by capillary wildness and osmotic hoopla. Antlers, when it can find them. No strong sense of destiny, looking good on it, and good looking.

COUNTRY GRIDDLE JESUS

Ply my sternum with a 2 by 4, sweet grandfather, that I may become one with the Country Griddle Jesus, whose sternum was plied to a puddle, so long ago. The shoulder blades . . . oh, my reality! Invoke metatarsal devastation on me, sire of my sire, that I might melt into the Country Griddle Jesus, whose metatarsals were made a wasteland. Make a loaf of me. Tread me down through bricks and history with your synthetic boots. Rake my skull 'cross a bed of hot dingo. I submit my hide to your morning star and your atlatl, your nunchuks and your stiletto heel.

DAY OLD JESUS

We live in the desert and we're falling down in anticipation. Our finger is on the switch, even when we fall down. The switch lights the applause sign. The Day Old Jesus is coming. He has agreed to pose for our applause, here among the jackbrush and demonthistle. We have devoted our water resources to remaining standing in the face of so much anticipation, but the burden has been too great. Can you help us in any way?

Director's Cut Jesus

The Director's Cut Jesus and his dead mathematics pupil were at the beach. The Director's Cut Jesus said, "I have put 500 gallons of poison into the water and you need to get them out." The Director's Cut Jesus's dead mathematics pupil rubbed his purple wrists together and said, "How is this a math problem?" But you should have seen the Director's Cut Jesus's dead mathematics pupil's mushy little head bowing before his master as he said this, and you should have seen him close his translucent eyelids, through which his irises could still be dimly seen. The Director's Cut Jesus's plumage flowed in the wind, parallel to the direction of the horizon, indicating what? Possibility?

Extended Warranty Jesus

The church building has a corner where its two walls come together. This place is what the Extended Warranty Jesus climbs down face first like a spider. No spider has a face. Look at him, again. He is climbing down the corner face first like a spider. Some spiders have some faces. Divine spiders have faces both great and terrible, with eyes that open out on a created world full of things to climb down face first like a spider. A spider has no face first.

EZ Bake Jesus

I've got a pushcart full of boomerangs and nobody's buying. Across the street, the EZ Bake Jesus is selling straight sticks. People are buying them like they're free. So here I am, trying to straighten out my boomerangs, and along comes a policeman, and smashes out the tail light of my pushcart with his nightstick. "Got a tail light out, there," he says. "Where did you buy that nightstick?" I ask him.

Freeze Dried Jesus

One of us was pretending to be Ascended, whatever that means.
We all wanted some fires to stamp out, like the good old days.
First the dancing-around, then the stamping-out, like the good
old days. The trolley commissioner, a certain Freeze Dried Jesus,
resigned his post. Whatever that means. Then it began to rain.
There were leftover pieces to the puzzles we'd already solved.
We thought, have we solved these puzzles too efficiently? We
wondered, is there any reason to panic?

Gold Taste Award Jesus

The Gold Taste Award Jesus was discovered in 1999 at a
women's leadership conference in Sunnyvale, California, and
died shortly after. He has had several volumes of his witty and
delightful writing posthumously published, including *Jesus in
the Beehive* (1999) and *Jungle Gym Jesus* (2000), as well as a
children's book, *The Littlest Jesus* (1999). His widow, three
children, and blind dog currently make their home in
Portsmouth, New Hampshire.

Heavy Duty Jesus

Tell me about the Heavy Duty Jesus. That was my father's
name. Meg was my father's name. What did your father do? He
was painted on the side of a B-52. Was he beautiful? Yes, he had
beautiful plumage. So did my father. Was he sexy? Yes I suppose
he was sexy. He had sexy plumage. The sexual emblem is
always the one painted on aircraft. Yes it is. I have dreams of a
different world. Dreams? Yes. Like visions? Yes. Like visions of
a different set of variables and constants? A whole new mess
of socio-economic nuts and bolts? Yes. And how are we to
identify the Heavy Duty Jesus in this alternate universe you see?
We will know him by the fruit he bears.

Honey Nut Jesus

I sent word to my love by pogo-courier that I lost my job:
"My dear Honey Nut Jesus—

I have lost my job at the fire hydrant factory, where I carved the
sand molds, as you know. I carved a pair of tits on a bunch of
fire hydrants, my love, because of your tits that I was thinking
about. My higher-ups were in tears, beholding the beauty of the
fire hydrants' tits. But fear not, I will be starting my new job as
a pogo-courier by delivering this message to you. Maybe you
will still love me?"

But as a pogo-courier, must I not also hold to the center, where
the tits are?

I Can't Believe It's Not Jesus

Only one episode of I Can't Believe It's Not Jesus has ever been
taped in the wild. In it, the I Can't Believe It's Not Jesus and his
wacky sidekick Buck are going to host a cooking show on the
cable access channel. The only recipe in the cookbook is a
recipe for a poking. Ingredients: one musket with bayonet, one
wacky sidekick. Grasp musket firmly. With a self-assured
stabbing motion, ventilate wacky sidekick. Repeat. And so the
cameras roll.

Improved Wheat Taste Jesus

The Improved Wheat Taste Jesus snoozes by a stack of ugly
little boxes with his feet stretched across the flow of sidewalk
traffic, so that the traffic slows down to read his sign:
Ugly Little Boxes
Made By a Klutz

INDUSTRIAL STRENGTH JESUS

If anyone ever tells you God doesn't deal in mass production tell that person to fuck off. Consider the lilies of the field and the sparrows of the air. The Industrial Strength Jesus is the moment at which a cloud of sparrows ignites and leaves the realm of the Bird Field Guide. When the little black eyes of too many sparrows are too close together the whole cloud ignites and burns. And what fuel does it consume. And at what temperature does it burn. And can it be extinguished.

INTRODUCING . . . JESUS

How does a child love another child? It must be a deadly secret. Like a deadly gas that escapes from between the teeth if the smile is too broad. The child must gestalt the other child, once, in the morning, during the taking off of backpacks: socks, flaxen hair, what have you. The child must take little sips of this total picture during the day. At recess, some chasing may occur. How does a child love the Introducing . . . Jesus? Smoothly, continually, like a swamp loves water. Like the electrician loves his feet and boots. Like the tree loves the negative space it enfolds in itself. Like the child loves to be loved, and loves to be saved.

JUST ADD WATER JESUS

The weather-control gun shorted out again. The Just Add Water Jesus kicked down the door wielding the gun-fixing gun. His plumage is primarily brown, but there are black spots. He has bunny ears and bunny teeth and a bunny tail. He looks very much like a chocolate bunny sprinkled with peppercorns emerging from the muzzle end of a chocolate and peppercorn feathered bunny gun.

Kids Eat Free Jesus

The Kids Eat Free Jesus locked himself in the bathroom, sat in the tub, took himself apart with a screwdriver. Why not, I thought. I got up to buy popcorn and soda. By the time I came back to my seat the house was burning down. I wrapped myself in wet towels and went to sleep. The Kids Eat Free Jesus woke me, and unwrapped me. You're a fireman! I said. Yes, said the Kids Eat Free Jesus, I am a fireman, now.

Kung Fu Grip Jesus

Then twilight. Doing the reverb thing. Providing the echo of itself in a sealed envelope in response to the question, "Where echo?" Providing it again. The Kung Fu Grip Jesus rides the slapback of the oncoming night, signifying basically the same thing again: "It is getting dark now, again." When those waves to ride are gone, it is ok to marinade in the unconscious for a while, the unimaginable unconscious of the Kung Fu Grip Jesus. Just not while the light is changing.

Lemon Scent Jesus

The rope that belongs to the Lemon Scent Jesus, now, will soon make a twisting sound. And from his promontory (every Lemon Scent Jesus comes with a free promontory) he sayeth the following, to his following, before his neck snappeth: "Blessed are the Saturdays, for they milkman unto heaven. Blessed egret odometer, for a blustery velvet pie. Blessed are they that toenail, for . . . "
Thus sayeth the Lemon Scent Jesus.

Limited Edition Jesus

The mating habits of the Limited Edition Jesus, I dare you.
First, the trip to buy the hover-belts and the other technology.
The striptease is of course the climax, and the writing of the
word STRIPTEASE on the mirror-room wall with the
genitalia-flavored lipstick. Then the philosophical inquiry into
the lipstick's irreducible truths. Then the song about the results
of the inquiry. Then the awareness of the results. Then the
results themselves: ten tiny Limited Edition Jesuses in their
original factory-sealed boxes.

Low APR Jesus

The talking bus is the one telling you to watch your mouth,
usually. There are stand-alone sentences, like monoliths, and
there are sentences meant to work with other sentences, like the
cells in a kitty cat's lung. The talking bus can do them all. It's
always tempting to put words into a character's mouth without
thinking, like I'm about to do with the talking bus. It helps fill
up space. I was going to do that with the Low APR Jesus, but
where is the necessity? The talking bus, now there's a thing that
needs to talk.

Mountain Spring Jesus

Jeremy and Todd, on the swingset. Jeremy's red windbreaker.
Todd chasing Beth, tripping over the concrete lizard's tail.
Jeremy and Todd turning Thanksgiving dinner into a food fight.
Todd pie face. Jeremy's scuffed elbows asleep. One corner of the
room. Scattered there. Reaction of Todd's parents. Todd's
parents chasing each other around the Christmas tree. Todd and
Jeremy's firetruck. A real fireman. Jeremy is a child hero. His
brown corduroy pants. Reaction of the Mountain Spring Jesus.
Todd's parents throwing mashed potatoes. Jeremy doing math

problems on his stubby fingers. Todd's piggyback rides. Todd's abacus. The wrapping paper around the abacus, the ribbon, the smell of fir needles, the same, same songs, the same.

No Risk Jesus

In the evening, when the sun was coughing up blood, the No Risk Jesus used all the parts of the animal. He made an orchestra. The resonant and stringy parts of the animal were used to make the instruments, and the squishy and talented parts were used to make the players, and one very special part was used to compose the symphony for the orchestra to play on itself. When the orchestra began to play, and the sun died for good, the No Risk Jesus grabbed his flamingo-leg shotgun and went out hunting, for another animal, for an audience.

Original Recipe Jesus

An excerpt from "I Was an Original Recipe Jesus":

"That was when the pouring happened. All the pouring happened in one sitting. At no time, once the pouring started, did it stop, until it stopped for good. A little lizard was underneath the pouring, and I said, 'Look out, small brother,' but the little lizard did not look out . . . As the powder of the pouring began to smother and cover him, and break his little bones, which are so much like our own, the little lizard asked me to stop the pouring, because of its oppressiveness, but I could not stop the pouring, because I was only an Original Recipe Jesus."

Over the Counter Jesus

It's no good. I keep smelling something else. The neighbors are pounding on the door. The police and fire officials are playing Jefferson Airplane on loudspeakers outside. The executioners' guild is on full alert. My guardian angel is chewing through his leg to get away and there's nothing I can do.

REDI-SERV JESUS

I want my Redi-Serv Jesus with his eyes on fire, all fierce and full of fuck. I want my Redi-Serv Jesus with an uzi in his mouth, protruding from his mouth, and his feet blazing like disease. Can my Redi-Serv Jesus know kickboxing? Can he be too bright to put in my living room? The apocalypse will not be a time, it will be a vicinity: his vicinity. All hail him, the Buoyant Face, the Hot Ingot Face. . . .

SWEET AND SOUR JESUS

Slinking over the cobblestone roads at night, straddling the drainage channel in the middle or hugging the dark wall, the Sweet and Sour Jesus makes his way from one den of iniquity to the next, like a desert creature between oases. He travels alone. He often pays for sex but turns the light off during. (Electric bill.) He often tells her to be on top. Of what importance? His nocturnal eyes are enlarged and enyellowed. The Sweet and Sour Jesus inspires loathing in his followers, and has very few followers.

THICK AND CHUNKY JESUS

The Thick and Chunky Jesus lives in a cave in the jungled-over part of the town. Squatting in a loincloth made of book leather, he nurses his belly to a full-grown size. "I feed my belly milk and pumpkins and beer," said one Thick and Chunky Jesus, during a field interview in the summer of 1966. The specimen was amiable and had no fears. Never woke up spinning and empty in the middle of the night. When the belly is fully grown, it leaves the Jesus to pursue its fortune, out in the wide world.

"Good-bye, belly! Don't make any mistakes! Don't step on any snakes! I have loved you so!"

Two-In-One Jesus

It's always a filibuster in the graveyard with the Two-In-One Jesus, always a gavel coming down, trying to find a permanent place to land. It's always a non-stop stream of words and tap tap tap trying to find an ear or a chink in the silence to squeeze into, to forestall the silence. You want to listen in on the filibuster, to marvel at and savor the ravings. You have been doing that. You are always doing that. That's what I meant when I said "always."

Conclusion

This is the conclusion. If you have any questions there will be a question and answer session in a couple of weeks. My throat is really sore and I'm going to go eat some soup. I'm hoping that the soup will make my throat feel better. A video game based on the Guide is in video arcades everywhere. The home version is dehydrated. Do not add water! Do not walk on the grass! And cetera. Thanks for reading. Keep your nose clean.

SECTION FOUR

Cycle Back, Return to Zero

Psychopath! Return to zero!
If you clung between the curtains
and the window like one hundred moths,
as meditative, as untiring, I might
begin to think of you as a segmented
ambassador from another world:
I would whisper things in your ears.
(Let the Moon and Earth collide.
Draw this, all this mess, in
like a wire through your eyehole,
just as you are known to do;
spool it like the tune of a song
that becomes more memorable as it grows longer.)
And I would never know if it was the puff
of my breath, or my this-worldly noise
that didn't ruffle you more than a step or two,
more than a flutter of your gelatin-silver wings,
before you returned to the zero state,
whatever that is, whatever that's like.

But who's segmented? Who fails to tire?
We're all the way we all are,
if only just barely:

me, in spite of this, holding a bucket
of sticky suds below the curtains, shaking,
gallons of you falling out, unbetrothed, almost
unaided by gravity, yeah right, as if gravity could fail,
psychopath, to aid a floundering into the hereafter.

Not Going to Repeat Myself
or
Jacob's Marimba

Psychopath! Return to zero!
I may have been talking to myself, thirty feet up
in the air, another ten feet to go
to a stormcloud the size of a cow heart
held in the armpit of the barn's eave,
coated inside and out with cold morning wasps.

Psychopath! Return to zero!
I probably said it out loud that time,
but didn't hear myself,
it wasn't me up there anymore,
it was me holding the ladder
as the volunteer fireman/house painter
tried to paint the barn gray.
The wasps were in the way.
As he sprayed their nest with poison,
and wet wasps fell like dead candy kisses
on my arms and body and all around me,
he called down, "What did you say?"

Well, I wasn't going to repeat myself,
with his boots sounding
from each rung
a hollow tone
all the way down
like he was descending Jacob's Marimba
arriving at last on the farmland and bodies with a crunch.

Upwards

Upwards of 40 whales beached themselves on
we didn't hear a sound, a phone
that night awake I sipped from a can

when the morning came and all that day the sun
ratcheted up one side of the sky
rolled down the other away from the shadows

of the mechanisms spraying, falling like water,
guilt is the only thing that hurts why is
walking space kept between these crisp black

life-size photographs of whales this fallow
beach of an afternoon? The sand is fruiting
footprints. The sun. If it were winter I

would be someone else, with other problems. But thank
Almighty God that I am a gull and a crow
present on the occasion of the tearing out

from a hole in a dead flesh wall a string of jellied blood
with my beak like a fire poker I fling it up
stuck in mid-air between my black

bird eye and the sun, which takes of
that red tissue and makes an ember,
or the tissue makes an ember of the sun

Science Fiction

The gold lion's moist yawn fell around the granite globe:
ivies grew there: mice, hiding gray in the corners, spiraled out:
hairy swaths of bison trampled flat the lion's tongue:
distant teeth sparkled and were navigated by.

And in all that time, kneeling, you nothing but blinked.
You spat a mouth filled with paint against the cave wall
where your hand was, and left a shadow there. Then
you pushed, straightened your elbow, came up off your knees.

Outside, where the galaxies sprawl past, you moved
your hand to pluck one, to pull it from its socket
and place it in your mouth, to fizz your saliva, blood, ink
(for every cavity of sanity is carved from the irrational around it).

But you were stung, bit. You couldn't push through or pull.
Back under the atmosphere, where your body fell,
a song was stopping up your throat, thickening
and cooling like rock, from red to gray, growing old.

Everything's Chin

I tickled everything under its chin,
taught it how to talk.

The tickling talking came out of my fingertip
and went into everything's chin.

My neighborhood glistened as if lacquered by
the water of a recent storm.

I danced down the street. The street said,
"Oh, oh, your dancing feet hurt us, we

are a fragile street, we feel as though
a storm has recently passed." The pink hatchlings,

oddments blown from the nests, said, "Oh,
oh, the thud of the street still hurts us,

the cracked glaze pains us,
your scritching fingertip is pain to us."

Man Plant

In this drinking glass I have one Pipe Organ Plant. In this drinking glass I have one Boomerang Plant. In this drinking glass I have one Umbilical Plant. The greenery sprouts like cancer all around me. Since I'm such an unbelievable botanist you may wonder why I don't drink out of a pie pan on the floor. You'd be right to wonder. Does not my shower cap prevent my turning into a plant myself you'd also be right to wonder.

Yes, I see the stripe going up the back of your leg. It's very nice. What I really want is some zero-gravity. The tendrils go haywire operating outside their frame of reference. No, it's just a figure of speech.

No, I've never been there, but the research shows plants are much braver than people. Also they get nauseated less often.

After issuing a few stage directions I am ready to proceed but they have all left. Just as well, I'm tremendously sleepy.

I sleep upside down. Half my head is under water and my dreams are like a baseball game in zero-gravity. . . .

Two Hawks Are Above Cambridge

Two hawks are above Cambridge.
See how they ellipse.

They're a kind of head,
like an airplane is a head drawn forward

into a wire, too continuous for filming.
The talons and landing gear
are a kind of silent mouth.

The hiccupping line of brick buildings
that cups the sky they fly in
is a kind of rectum.

We're being driven forward through the snow
by a kind of disappointment or a kind of whip
that takes samples from our nerve cords

and trades them in for more continuous samples
and replaces them, the same way the hawks

get replaced: the air is a game.
It's different from the air we breathe.

Neighborhood Rubbed Raw

The 81st hated me and told me so.
Why do you lie to one who loves you so.
The Christmas came and went like a sack
of brown bread falling past an open window.

Late at night with the curtains pulled back
I stuck out my head in a burlap sack
and breathed in what air I could find.
The 81st frowned like a watermelon rind,

pulled me back in through a life-size egg slicer,
coughed up my constellation on the coffee table,
poured me out through a crystal stopper,
skewered me through the ankles with a helicopter—

that's right—as if the cracks between the floor
boards were capable of holding me and not one more.

I Don't Mind Failure

I don't mind failure so
the nickel stays half-cruxed

the mimetic buttonhole
the shoulders carry a tabletop

powder's falling again
she walked past her eyes rang up
no tensor was more fragile the
lumbered cross molten and
the brainchild cross-beams cracked

New here stop your
which you had
the frank detri-

allow wick most
who'll with
nectar be-
labored redoubled

O Grassy
O Daily Bird

And Because the Leaves Were On Strike

It was because all those racehorse clouds
trotted out my mouth in that ice air.

I reached up because the bird was singing,
pinched and pulled the thread of its song,
because, as I said, my voice was cold,
maybe a little lonely, and

when I pulled, it all came loose.
I was low, low.
Buried under a pile of red unraveled songbird.

What really happened was
I was just standing there breathing,
and there were 20,000 birds,
starlings, way up above my reach,
perched like leaves, where no leaves were,
because of the strike,
and boiling and howling, all of them.
When they made up their mind to stop, all at once,
I had nothing to do with it. Somehow.

In Silence

In silence bit my lower lip harder.
The brook unrolls like a roll of paper.
Ten of us spat games onto the other.
In silence bit my lower lip harder.

The brook unrolls like a roll of paper.
Let her fill the white pages after.
Blackly broken in circumference together.
The brook unrolls like a roll of paper.

Let her fill the white pages after.
In silence bit my lower lip harder.
I tilt, eyes pour imperfect water.
Let her fill the white pages after.

SECTION FIVE

What I Can Make Out From Here

They're writing in the sand.
They're writing, "How thin a thread the beach is.
        Why, I can hardly stand on it.
        And yet, history teaches,
        Explorers always land on it,
        Because it has so much sand on it."
One of them is a porcelain outline.
Sir Isaac Newton, the bulldog,
is fascinated with her.
Her face keeps almost making him reinvent calculus,
because of how curvy it is.
He licks her more gently than a tulip.
It's a still-life. I hate still-lifes.
I like the dog though because he won't sit still.
In the painting there are a thousand tongues
all over the porcelain one's egglike outline:
we're seeing a strap of time.
The words they wrote are written near there.
(Not anymore, really, of course.)
The rest of it is boring.
Each has a red wheel for a head.
Their heads aren't even turning.

Note, Too, the Canny Musk

The trombone flower lifts her lung-ache
up into the morning air
which is itself a cold dead alloy.

All around her, the aluminum desert floor
begins to stink as the sun
does its best bulldozer since yesterday
when the temperature was a mile wide

with teeth evaporation-sized.
The trombone flower lives slow.
That's the secret.

What does the trombone flower say?
Broo. That's all.
Broo, broo, broo. Then some hours.
The sun turns off and right back on again.

Not Peel

If the door to your house is unlocked
it's very much like I'm already inside
and if the water is on inside your house
then it's very much like I'm already in the water
playing among the fishes and sea-mammals
that are already very much like inside your house.

What about honey? Honey happens when a bee
takes nectar and enzymes and lets them react.
Is there honey in your house? One way to find out
would be to look for nectar, enzymes, a bee,
and time in your house.

Let's not peel the wallpaper too literally
even if passion demands that our fingers
become talons and attack your house
from the inside which is very much like the outside.
You lying naked on your back in your bed.
A powerful thing leaving your muscles, kissing my head.

You, lying breasts exposed to the air,
words and breath stumbling like drunk,
after a peak, biting my chin
like taking chocolate off a strawberry.
Barely choosing what things get said.

Wichita, Kansas

We held hardened sepals under our tongues.
Our brainstems were pinched.

My Mindy and myself.
We watched all day.
What the tornado did four houses down.

The dogs gathered in the mess
and trash left of the house

three houses down, eating, mouths
downward, rib cages breathing. The dandelion
factory, and those clowns that run it,

next door, my mother kept saying, but a chimney
was always breaking loose in sorrow,

losing its mooring and its address,
drifting and curling away
toward Io, moon of Jupiter, by this time of night

just a slim crescent cut from the sky
by a boy with winged shoes and

a scalpel. This makes us believe
in what a sliver can begin as.
I don't recall how it all went,

but for my first tactile moment with you
under a thunderous gardenia,

blue-eyed, green-eyed,
and everywhere we pressed down with my thumb
it took root, the pectin spreading

like jackfrost into the fields that surrounded,
held us infinitely, and a barn, and the barn lifting, pushing

off with its snail-foot, following the line
a bed-sheet might take
if it were suddenly acknowledged a saint.

The Dark Room

There is a green scratch, right down the middle of her face, and I can't tell if the negative was scratched intentionally or unintentionally. The two guitar soundholes which are her eyes—if you run a straight line through the center of each, and another straight line through the tips of the little pink volcanoes on her breasts, you'll see that these two lines are almost never parallel, though they do stay in the same plane. Since they're not parallel, they meet at some point, and that point where they meet is in the room, and as she moves slowly, like a cat being cleaned, the point moves slowly, a little moth of light projected onto the walls and doors of the room, by her catlikeness. The point where the lines meet is moving harmonically, tracing and retracing the same path, because she herself is moving harmonically, and rhythmically. The point is tracing the shape of a half moon. Her movement is informed by the upper/lower split of her eyes and her breasts, that's what her eyes and breasts tell me. The upper and lower halves, split by the imaginary lines, push on each other, like foreground and background, like I'm pushing on her breasts with my hands, because it feels like the right thing to do, to correspond with whatever is inside her, pushing against her eyes, which I can see happening. The various pushings push on each other and mix like colors of paint, chase each other like cats and moths. The orange light is striped across us with black in between it.

It may be her trying to ignore the green scratch in the room that's telling in her eyes. I'm trying to ignore it too. Her eyes seem to be getting larger. Her eyes are giving way to my whole body now, I can stand up in them, I could fall silent in here, I have already fallen silent.

Nonsense

"Nonsense makes the heart grow Blonder," she giggled, hanging
as if halfway out of a haystack, red blouse half undone, hay stuck
to her chest, mouth, neck.

"I saw that you were distracted,
looking at the flowers by the exit ramp," I told her.
"I should've said something."

If faces pitch, hers pitched
with whimsy.

"They were such a beautiful red, like brake lights
and sports cars and stop
signs all rolled together."

I said, "My love, you and I have just had a very serious
accident; look at the lights and sirens
bouncing off your skin even now!"

She said, "They're beautiful, aren't they? My wilted body,
my floral blood, spread across the canvas of the road, mingling
with the common glass and wreckage, that they might be saved."

Dot

Little bright blue pores: pills and
jewels dot the green land-rush of your skin.

To make an angel, somebody sticks wings in.
Like pushing quills into a ball of dough.

My arms are made like a wingspan.
My back and shoulders darker than blue.

My neck is outer space.
Inside my brain, twisting and craning to hold you.

Mister Goodbye Easter Island

(There are not enough trees there
for even one day's life rafts.) He knows
how thick, how taut inside the stone,
knows the half-burial, inwardly attending,
knows the island a flat projection
of his own globe, all awareness facing the core
toward a bone that was wrenched
and bleached and buried there
at the pit of a bald land, to bake
under a silent, collective stare.
What good would good do
one who knows these things?
The obsidian of their eyes crackles,
the air there sings.

Recent Titles from Alice James Books

The Devil's Garden, Adrian Matejka
The Wind, Master Cherry, the Wind, Larissa Szporluk
North True South Bright, Dan Beachy-Quick
My Mojave, Donald Revell
Granted, Mary Szybist
Sails the Wind Left Behind, Alessandra Lynch
Sea Gate, Jocelyn Emerson
An Ordinary Day, Xue Di
The Captain Lands in Paradise, Sarah Manguso
Ladder Music, Ellen Doré Watson
Self and Simulacra, Liz Waldner
Live Feed, Tom Thompson
The Chime, Cort Day
Utopic, Claudia Keelan
Pity the Bathtub Its Forced Embrace of the Human Form,
   Matthea Harvey
Isthmus, Alice Jones
The Arrival of the Future, B.H. Fairchild
The Kingdom of the Subjunctive, Suzanne Wise
Camera Lyrica, Amy Newman
How I Got Lost So Close to Home, Amy Dryansky
Zero Gravity, Eric Gamalinda
Fire & Flower, Laura Kasischke
The Groundnote, Janet Kaplan
An Ark of Sorts, Celia Gilbert
The Way Out, Lisa Sewell
The Art of the Lathe, B.H. Fairchild
Generation, Sharon Kraus
Journey Fruit, Kinereth Gensler
We Live in Bodies, Ellen Doré Watson
Middle Kingdom, Adrienne Su
Heavy Grace, Robert Cording
Proofreading the Histories, Nora Mitchell
We Have Gone to the Beach, Cynthia Huntington
The Wanderer King, Theodore Deppe
Girl Hurt, E.J. Miller Laino
The Moon Reflected Fire, Doug Anderson

ALICE JAMES BOOKS has been publishing exclusively poetry since 1973. One of the few presses in the country that is run collectively, the cooperative selects manuscripts for publication through both regional and national annual competitions. New regional authors become active members of the cooperative, participating in the editorial decisions of the press. The press, which historically placed an emphasis on publishing women poets, was named for Alice James, sister of William and Henry, whose fine journal and gift for writing went unrecognized within her lifetime.

Typeset and Designed by Dede Cummings
Printed by Thomson-Shore